THIS THING THAT IS NOT A THING

This Thing That Is Not A Thing

Poems by Paulette A. Ramsay

Canoe Press

Jamaica • Barbados • Trinidad and Tobago

Canoe Press
7A Gibraltar Hall Road, Mona
Kingston 7, Jamaica
www.uwipress.com

A catalogue record of this book is available from the
National Library of Jamaica.

ISBN: 978-976-653-025-9 (paper)
978-976-653-026-6 (Kindle)
978-976-653-027-3 (ePub)

Cover image by Marcel Messam
Cover and book design by Robert Harris
Set in Gandhi Serif 10/14
Printed in the United States of America

Contents

THIS THING THAT IS A THING . . .

This Thing That Is Not a Thing

how does this thing end
this thing that has me trapped
in the middle of its web
ongoing but stagnant
persistent but dead
who will end this thing
that keeps
pretending to be a real thing

this thing is like a flour dumpling
in a big pot of Jamaican soup
boiling boiling boiling
without steam
the yam doan want it beside it
the coco doan want it beside it
but it keep rolling aroun an aroun
in the bubbling soup
the soup bubbling over
splashing all over the stove
is not a real fire
the dumpling keep rolling aroun and aroun

this thing is not a thing
pretending it is a thing
everybody thinks it is a thing
but it is not a thing
it is no thing
it is nothing.

I Know I'm Not Supposed to Tell You

you could tell me
even if I didn't ask
even if I didn't want you to tell me
no one would be bothered if you told me
and even if you could read my mind
and see it
right there
I should hide it
not make it obvious
that this is a thing for me

you would say
you're supposed to put those thoughts
in my mind
you would want to know
you could depend on me
to think the way you would want me to
you would want me to know
that it was your eyes
that made me think that way
you would want to know
that I will only respond
to your eyes

even before I begin to think
you would have to know
that you could trust me
to understand only you can make it a thing
to let you
allow me to think

about you
like that
or even at all . . .

When Women Don't Speak

when women speak their minds
they are problematic, subversive
men who speak their minds
are simply expressing concerns,
when women suggest
there is an absence of fairness
they are pugnacious, not tame
when men express same
they are measured, appropriate, logical

when women ask probing questions
they are mischief makers
stirring up trouble
when men ask the same questions
they are brilliant
critical thinkers

that's the reason women
sometimes say *absolutamente nada*
nutten, nothing
just sit and watch them,
listen to them
do serious damage to words.

I Do Not Want to Do It

do not try to make me do it
I do not want to do it
I do not like it
I am not interested in it

    it is not fair
    to ask me to do this thing
    my mind is not in it
    my heart is not in it
    I can imagine no pleasure in it

I will not do this thing
I will NOT take a slingshot
and shoot stupid men between their legs!

THORNBIRD

you are my thornbird
my singular source of rapture
now, as you were
in the beginning
the one
I see
amidst a flock
of a thousand others
I am your forever birdwatcher
from the edges
of cliffs
from the banks of rivers
I watch as you soar
spread your wings, dodge,
cumbersome clouds
glide through blue skies

I watched
as others
more skilful
trapped you
briefly, even in broken nets
once I heard
a catapult's stone
brought
you
  to
   the
     ground
you healed yourself

and flew away
before I got to you.

Sometimes
I'm sure
you're headed
straight
toward my outstretched hands
I wait for you
to flap your wings
and land
on my hands
on my shoulder
even on my head
but as you
get close to me
you soar high
above my head
and seek refuge
in the clouds
again and again.

I watch you now and smile
take pleasure
in seeing you soar
dodge the clouds
fly above my head
make me believe
you see my outstretched hands
fly around me
away from me
show the strength of your wings
making me think
one day
I could climb on them

and fly with you away
from the edge
of the cliff.

(Adapted from the poem in *Under Basil Leaves: An Anthology of Poems* [London: Hansib, 2010].)

IF YOU COULD

If you could
strip away
the layers of my mind
and see what I think
about these things
you would certainly be shocked

If you could
strip away
the layers of my mind
and see what I really think
about this thing
and that thing
you would probably die

perhaps if I could
strip away the layers
of your mind
and see what you think
about this thing
I would drop dead too.

PUTTING BRAKES ON ME

I feel myself
slowly slipping
back into that deep hole
present and past pushing
against each other
alter ego
clamouring for attention
tired of being suppressed
by this thing
but I will not let myself fall
I will laugh
for me, for you
with you
just laugh and sing
to save me
from falling
back into that deep hole
just because of this thing
that you did . . .
though you think it is not a thing . . .

YOU DISTURBED MY DREAMS

I am still disturbed
by the bold way
you interrupted
my dream

you chased away
my friends
who had come to see me
celebrate another birthday
Papa was there
Gertrude was there
Johnny, Tony, Auntie P
even Sue who left
two weeks ago

I thought
you brought good luck
but just before I hugged you
you turned into a slithering snake
and slid away
with my best friend
on your tail
first you surprise me
then you make me
angry
never show yourself
to me again
neither real
nor imagined . . .

GUILTY LOVE

had to shame you
jook you in you eye
to make you
love me, like me even
it didn't have to happen, like that
you just needed to
see beyond my black skin
like me just because
I am flesh and blood
like you
like me for me
you love me now
cause you don't want
to feel shame . . .
shame on you
for shaming yourself
over a thing like that.

The Library

no one
can explain
why the students come to the library
but they keep coming
everyday
without fail
they sit all day
without fail
engage in empty chatter
without fail
there are no books
in this place of erudition
there are no books
in this place of information
on the topics
they chat and shout about
all day . . .
still they come . . .
'tis a mystery.

The Mother of an Addict Speaks

every day guilt gnaws at my insides
like a starving rat
its my fault
I was excessive with indulgences
smiled at his deviance

still, I took him to Sunday school
till he was twelve
showed him Jesus, the Cross
and the Bible
no, it's his fault
he's twenty four, not twelve
I will not carry guilt that belongs to him
I will look at his madness,
his decrepit body, his vacant eyes
still I ask
did I leave things unsaid, undone?
did he forget things I said?

this thing that gnaws like
a voracious rat at my guts
is all his fault
he chose it
but I swear
I'll kill this thing
that is making him into
nothing
with my bare mother's hands
one day.

Human Rights

we all have rights
they say
human rights
right to do so and so
right to say so and so
right to live
right to eat

some fight to show
their rights
some fight to show
this thing called
human rights is not a thing
for all
for some, not all
should not speak
should not do
or even be . . .
what a thing . . .

Jamaican Ugly Man Syndrome

one tooth in de mouth
dat God give him
one twist up twist up tooth
like ficus root
one eye
face look like S
but him tink him nice

so you in a hardware store
for example
you know say you look good
you know say you just a dazzle
in your brand new stretch Levi
or whatever brand you prefer
you buying your bowl
for your Saturday soup
a one tooth
ben-up foot S-face man
come tell you
yes dat is a nice one
yuh civilise so yuh jus smile
him walk off, then turn back an
say dat one is my size
I can come for soup dis evening

of course
de bowl drop out a yuh han and bruk
yuh look on him an yuh
open yuh mout and close it
yuh don't know if yuh fi sorry

for him or vex with him
yuh ask him yuh have a mirror
him seh yes, mi have mirror
yuh shake yuh head
yuh know is a sign of Jamaican
ugly man syndrome
de uglier dem be
de more familiar dem be
cause there is not one Jamaican
ugly man
dat know or believe
dat him is ugly

every Jamaican man
street boy, mad man
hungry man
bruk foot man
tink him full eye
you ever see how mad man
eye light up
if yuh full eye
is true
gully man or rat man
tink him can get any woman

for dere is not one Jamaican
ugly man who tink him is ugly.

Marcus Garvey in Cuba

(For Jamaican descendants in Cuba)

Marcus Mosiah Garvey
went to Prescott and Banes,
in every corner
Jamaicans waited
to hear this Jamaican man
some say is a prophet
some say a fool
some say is a Jamaican
who don't want to come here
and work like we
chop cane like we
put down iron like we
so he preach to we
tell we go back to Africa
but him don't tell we
if we should go back
to Jamaica first
and then go to Africa
him don't tell we
what we will do in Africa
an him doan't habla spaniol either
they shake dem heads
suck dem teet
built a UNIA centre
and repeated Garvey's
back to Africa message everyday.

If Nicolás Guillén Came to Cuba Today

where would he go?
to his beloved Camagüey?
to the Malecón?
to contemplate el Mar Caribe?
to the *zafra* to smell
the sweet scent of sugarcane?
would he dust off his retired typewriter
type a new page
about Cuba today?

if Nicolás Guillén came to Cuba today?
what would he say
to black women
in short short mini skirts
cleaning floors in Hotel Nacional?
what would he say
to old black men, weak and reed-like
straining against the weight
of the rickety handcarts
they push
through the streets of Havana?

what would he say
to young black boys
panting and puffing
as they pedal cycle taxis
up steep hills, across bumpy roads
to help curious tourists see Havana.

would Guillén
write a new version of "Tengo"?
would he sit and read
his favourite lines
from his many tomes?
what would he say
if he knew that
some now say *sí tengo,*
pero quiero . . . quiero . . . ?
what music would he dance to?
el Changüí?
la rumba?
la tumba francesa?
la salsa?

what instruments would
he want to hear
as he moved to sharp Cuban rhythms,
los cascabeles
las marímbulas
las maracas o el güiro?
Nicolás Guillén should come to Cuba today
and write a new version of "Tengo".

You are Not a Bright Socialist

what you did
when you tried
to use your preponderous gut
to push me off the edge
where you saw me
(I was sure
I was not there
I was
in fact,
in conversation
with two bright men
about centre-margin matters)
is unpardonable
that is the reason I jooked you
in the middle of the dirty blue of your eyes.
—*Perdón, buenos días señor*

I watched with glee
your face
go from yellow to red, to pink, to red
to purple
I know you did not know
what to think or do
or you would move your heavy gut
off my arm
stop trying to topple me
with the force of lard
cómo estás you stutter
muy bien I condescend
thinking, I got you this time
and you didn't even do it with class
you ugly, clueless worm!

MEMORIES OF MY GIRLHOOD

laughter
bubbling happily like water from a hot spring
hibiscus hedges, my best friends
their flowers eagerly adorn my thick plaits
sweet cashew juice dripping from my elbows
custard apples, rose apples and Julie mangoes
that nobody owned
open pastures with cows no one feared
we loved their milk
thick cream and hot foam
like a frill, frothing at the top of our cups
kind neighbours with children who said good evening
and thank you ma'am
boys and girls playing handball
Anansi stories in the moonlight
homework that was fun to do
homework that made me
happy
homework that made me
think
homework that made me
hurry to school next day
to show off the gems I discovered last night
adults who were my keepers
unforgettable moments residing in my head.

Your Plan

you shocked me
by the speed
with which you
stabbed me in the back
of my neck
the minute I turned around . . .
I never saw the knife
you'd kept hidden
all the time
I called you my friend . . .
you'd even kissed me
like Judas kissed Jesus
others watched you smile
with me
no one suspected your plan . . .
the thing I thought was our thing
was really not ever a thing

WHEN OOMAN BADMINDED

dem will kill you
with one lie
mash you up for life
step over you, like you dead
believe me
a badmimded ooman is more dangerous
than an armed gunman . . .
more dangerous
than a pitbull
just dangerous
very dangerous
very very dangerous . . .

Tek Back Yuh Ole Bruk

Papa's old Austin Cambridge
huffed and puffed
groaned and moaned
as it crawled into the garage
we ran out to greet him
but more so to get a toffee for me
a lollipop for Junior
a penny-shaped bubble gum for Gee
a paradise plum for Bee
the things he brought home in his pockets
were always more enticing to us
than his half-smiling face

this day was different
he quietly opened the trunk
pointed to the parcel
he had collected at the Post Office
"Parcel from Englan," he said
half-tired, half-impressed
we were very impressed
our eyes opened wide
as we looked at the big box
wrapped in brown paper
and half covered in stamps
with the face of Missis Queen
as Mama used to say
and our Aunt's firm teacher-like cursive
Mr. J.L. Hoffstead
Biggersteth P.O., Jamaica W.I.

Our eyes opened wide
parcel come we whispered
parcel come
just loud enough to hear each other
but soft enough so Papa
wouldn't scold us for over-eagerness
(so strict and proper he was)
finally we had got our own parcel
like our friends
who always showed off new shoes, new frock,
pretty things they got in parcel
(sometimes they were ugly)

Papa picked up the huge box
and grunted on discovering
it wasn't light
we ran behind him
as he struggled to take the clumsy box
into the house

Mama came into the living room
as he put the box on the floor
bring the scissors
she pointed to us children
as she sat down and her eyes got
shiny and bright with expectation
we all gathered around and watched
Papa cut away brown paper
and carton snip snip scrunch scrunch
jaws dropped in unison
loud gasps escaped our six mouths

Papa said nothing
Mama opened her mouth and clapped it shut
Gee said, "Ole shoes . . ."
Sue said, "Ole clothes!"
"Shush!" Mama said. "The neighbours
will hear!"

Papa sank his forklift hands
deep into the box
we watched limp string after limp string
fall back into the space
seeking refuge in its ample depth
Papa said not a word
he quietly closed the box
"Pass me a pen and paper,"
he said dryly
then he sat and wrote in big bold letters
"My dear Sister Vie, tek back yuh ole bruk."
He folded the paper neatly
gently put it on top of the rags.
"Tomorrow I will post the box right back
to my sister in Englan," he said quietly
as if it was just the right thing to do

"Dinner time," he said, rubbing his hands
looking relieved in his face.
"Wife, what you cook today?"
"A nice piece of Butcher Guthrie steak."
"Alright," Papa said. "Alright."
"Steak time!"
"Come we sit an eat good good Jamaican steak.
No ole bruk from Englan for we!"

Questions for a Departed Loved One

why you go and do a thing like that?
jus drop dead like that . . .
without a word of warning
why you do that?
you keep that as secret?
so only you and the Man up top
know about dis ting?
how long
him really tell you?
you keep it as big secret?
or you did get
last minute notice too?

My Uncle Said Goodbye Today

wondering why
my uncle decide to drop out today
of all days
this week of all weeks
why not last month
or two months from now
but now when I have
so many things to do
bills to pay
house to paint
just buy a new car
and a new apartment
this is not a convenient time
at all

have no money
to pay for wake, pay for repast
at hotel, glass casket and all
those things dat he say he want
leave long list with orders
who must be pallbearer
who must sing
who must not dare to sing (for they can't sing)
who must preach
who must not preach (for they can't preach)
who must do eulogy (for they write and spell well . . .)

all of that is fine
but he should really pick
a better time to go
make it easier for me

to help send him off in style
according to his orders
send me home in style
him have no money
to sen home himself in style
and I have none
to sen him home in style
but when all is said and done
I have to bury him
bury him, bury him
all of him
good and proper . . .

THIS THING THAT IS A THING . . .

Things Black and Beautiful

the poetry of Nicolás Guillén
Langston Hughes, Nancy Morejón
Cristina Cabral, Shirley Campbell
Cos Causse

"unequivocally black"
"unequivocally beautiful"

the ackee seed
the twittering blackbird

your hair
your face
my sister's hips
my sister's lips

your nose
your lips
all of you

your black face
the music of Aretha Franklin
Me.

Self-liberation

spurn guilt
after you have used up
all your ink
on words which tell too much,
sit in secret places
in crusty old dresser drawers
waiting to be read
it takes a long time to figure out
the meaning of this
me, you
a broken vase
held together by crazy glue
so out of place
on my grandmother's mahogany table
reflecting the cracks in the ceiling
speak audibly
and then say no more.

(Adapted from the poem in *October Afternoon* [London: Hansib, 2012].)

PRAYER FOR OUR WORLD

Lord,
evil without restraint stalks the earth
someone spilled a phial
and let the demons out
they roam
like roaring lions
like sin
from the gut of hell itself
like chaff
which the wind puffs
all over
but Your righteousness
Jehovah Tsidkenu
can cover evil
trample evil
deliver us from evil
or we perish
deliver us from evil
or we die
for Thine is the Kingdom
and the glory
forever, and ever
Amen.

DAILY PRAYER

Good morning Lord,
thank You for
using that noisy blackbird
to wake me up today
You know
I really hate croaking lizards
but I still don't mind
that sound that You used yesterday
to wake me up

to wake up
is to delight in Your goodness
to wake up new every morning
is to witness anew the world announce Your glory
I will not ask You
to protect me today
I will not ask You for food
I will not ask You
for friends
I will just say thank You Lord
for being an awesome Provider, Friend,
Protector and Guide.

The Love of God

I know of no words
in any dictionaries
in any encyclopaedias
in any books at all
or in my mind to fully
tell you
of the love of God
its depth, its height
its unconditionality and persistence
its complexity and simplicity
its compassion and urging power
its warmth
its life-saving force
its healing force
not my tiny mind
not your finite one
can tell the
fullness of this love
that's without comparison
vast, unending
available . . .

REQUIEM FOR A VICTOR

(*For Shelly, Becky and Joyce*)

Dear Santita,
It was easy, uncomplicated
loving you, that is
you made elegance desirable
discretion appealing
altruism admirable
honesty calming, endearing
complex you were, but uncomplicated
calm, but intensely courageous
and how you cherished your Shelley,
your sibilings, family, all
taught us to open our hearts to love

surgery after surgery, treatment after treatment
you gritted your teeth
climbed the stairs to JMMB
showed the meaning of resilience
your faith, the substance of things you hoped for
we witnessed your spiritual growth
your quiet, dignified fight, resistance
to the vicious assault
on your body

Jehovah Tsidkenu was with you
He restored your soul
renewed your mind
you believed His promise
you joined Him in a covenant
that will never be forgotten
either way you would be a winner

and though the untameable thing roared like a lion,
plundered your physical being,
Jehovah Rapha healed your soul

truth is
you really never stopped for death
you had learnt a long time ago
that it would walk with anyone
talk with anyone
smile with anyone
and rob everyone
true,
it tried to stop you
ingratiated itself on you
but it never expected the quiet
fight of steel

Jehovah Shammah was with you
keeping you in perfect peace
holding you,
walking with you
as you kept your mind on Him
you jabbed the vile thing in the eyes
in your quiet fight
that degenerate thing never met a girl like you!

Throughout the days, weeks, months and years
time that seemed to merge into one long blur
you kept your eyes on Jehovah Tsidkenu
when the vicious thing cornered you
in the desert place
you drew water from the wells of salvation
and they never went dry

long before they closed this box
long before they decided on a spot
long before they made the first call
long before they pulled the sheets
you had stepped into the Promised Land
you stood before Him saying,
"You are awesome!
You are awesome!"

I see you now
in full abandonment
rapt adoration
embrace the fulfilment
of the promise, in this land
where there is no fear
no pain, just peace
that passeth all understanding
as you traverse this land
your only words
"Holy, Holy, Holy!
I worship You!
I worship You!"

Jehovah Rapha healed your soul
you join the angels,
a victor
Jehovah Rapha healed your soul
you are a victor
Jehovah Sabaoth, the Lord of Hosts beckoned
saying, "Enough, my child, come.
Enter into the Holy Place!"
Jehovah Tsidkenu has been your Restorer
Jehovah Rapha has healed your soul
and made you whole
and now you sing, "It is well, it is well
with my soul."

you will rest in peace my friend
Jehovah Shalom is your peace
Jehovah Shammah has never left you
Jehovah Tsidkenu is your all
they will lay this box gently
but you, you are long resting
in the land of peace
declaring, "I am standing on Holy Ground!"
Jehovah Rapha healed your soul
Jehovah Shalom is your peace
Jehovah Nissi your Banner in the fight
yours is the victory!
yours is the joy!
in the presence of the Great I AM.
You declare
"How great Thou art!
How great Thou art!"

(Written for the thanksgiving service of my beautiful friend Santita, January 2018.)

Acknowledgements

Thanks to all those persons, including Lisa Brown, Shavelle Smith and especially Shavelle, who helped to make this possible. Thanks to Keilah Mills for her eagle eyes and editorial patience. Thanks to the University of the West Indies Press/Canoe Press and all reviewers and critics of this collection.

Other books by Paulette A. Ramsay

- *Construcciones afromexicanas de diáspora, género, identidad y nación* (Kingston: University of the West Indies Press, 2020)
- *Star Apple Blue and Avocado Green* (Kingston: Ian Randle, 2017)
- *Afro-Mexican Constructions of Diaspora: Gender, Identity and Nation* (Kingston: University of the West Indies Press, 2016)
- *October Afternoon* (London: Hansib, 2012)
- *Under Basil Leaves: An Anthology of Poems* (London: Hansib, 2010)
- *Alles Liebe, deine Sunshine: eine Erzählung in Briefen aus Jamaika* (Zurich: Atlantis Verlag, 2005)
- *Aunt Jen* (London: Heinemann, 2002)

Co-authored books

- *The Afro-Hispanic Reader and Anthology*, by Paulette A. Ramsay and Antonio D. Tillis (Kingston: Ian Randle, 2018)
- *Español Avanzado*, by A. Bankay, Paulette A. Ramsay and J. Williams (Kingston: Ian Randle, 2013)
- *Blooming with the Poius: A Rhetorical Reader for Caribbean Tertiary Students*, by Paulette A. Ramsay, Vivienne A. Harding, Janice A. Cools and Ingrid A. McLaren (Kingston: Ian Randle, 2008)
- *Cheveré: Spanish for Caribbean Secondary Schools*, books 1, 2 and 4, by Paulette A. Ramsay, et al. (Essex, UK: Pearson, 2005)
- *Between Two Silences: Translated Short Stories of Hilma Contreras*, by Paulette A. Ramsay and Anne-María Bankay (Kingston: Arawak, 2004)
- *Practice Papers for CXC Spanish*, by Paulette A. Ramsay and Anne-María Bankay (Kingston: LMH Publishers, 1999)
- *On Friday Night*, translated novel of Luz Argentina Chiriboga by Paulette A. Ramsay and Anne-María Bankay (Kingston: LMH Publishers, 1998)

CPSIA information can be obtained
at www.ICGtesting.com
Printed in the USA
LVHW032019181221
706581LV00006B/365

9 789766 530259